THE CASE OF RAHEEL SIDDIQUI

The United States Marine Corps is renowned for its incredibly tight-knit culture, a bond that is unbreakable and unwavering. This unyielding commitment is perfectly encapsulated in their powerful motto, 'Semper Fidelis,' which resonates with profound emotional intensity - a constant reminder to remain forever faithful, no matter the challenges that may arise. At just 20 years old, Raheel Siddiqui was desperately searching for his next move in life. Filled with passion and determination, this exceptional student made the heart-wrenching decision to enlist in the Marine Corps, knowing deep in his soul that it was the perfect path to chase his dreams and honor his beloved country.

© 2023 [Jeffrey C. Mason]

TABLE OF CONTENTS
THE CASE OF RAHEEL SIDDIQUI   1

The Marine Corps is the smallest conventional military force in the United States. As of 2022, it has approximately 177,000 active-duty members and about 32 and a half thousand personnel in reserve. The Marine's motto, Semper fidelis, is a nod to the tight knit culture the Corps is known for. Meaning always faithful. The Latin phrase refers to the loyalty Marines have to their country, to their work, and to each other. In 2017. New York Times journalist Janet Reitman described them as having a tight bond grown out of the codes, traditions, and reverence for suffering that marines believe set them apart from civilians and all other military branches.

All enlisted female recruits and male recruits who reside east of the Mississippi river undergo their training at the Paris island recruit bow. Located on Port Royal Island in South Carolina, this military installation is where roughly 17,000 marines are trained each year. During the 13 week long training program, recruits are cut off from the outside world and undergo a physically and mentally grueling regimen. There are four battalions at Paris island which recruits are assigned to according to their platoon and company. The third recruit training battalion has a particularly imposing history. It's been described as attracting drill instructors with type A personalities who aim to build the most disciplined marines.

The third battalion's reputation is so notorious that it has been nicknamed. The 19 year old Jake Weaver was following in a family tradition when he enlisted in the marines. His grandfather had served in the Korean war in the early 1950s. In early 2015, Jake and his fellow recruits boarded the bus that would take them to Paris Island for their training. As soon as they arrived at their destination, they were met by a drill instructor who barked an order at them. Get on the yellow footprints. A long line of footprints had been painted along the asphalt nearby, marking a pathway to the entrance building. Following the instructor's orders, the recruits made their way towards the building to begin their training. Scenes inside the building were chaotic. Drill instructors bellowed at the recruits from all across the room as they filled out their intake forms and phoned their families. Recruits were permitted one call home no longer than 4 seconds and reciting a strict script.

After identifying themselves, they were to say, I have arrived safely at Paris Island. Please do not send any food or bulky items to me in the mail. I will contact you in seven to nine days by letter with my new address. Thank you for your support. Goodbye for now. Over the next few days, they were given uniforms. Their heads were shaved, physical fitness tests were taken, and then the real training could begin. Jake Weaver was assigned to Platoon 3054 in Lima

Company, which was assigned to the Third Battalion. When he and his fellow platoon mates met their drill instructors, the young recruits were asked a question. And you want to be trained like marines, right? Not like crappy individual marines. It would soon become clear what the dis meant by this. While some drill instructors were older, others were close in age to the recruits themselves. The majority of them hasn't served in combat, but instead works for the Marines as air traffic controllers, mechanics or technicians, amongst other roles. In order to become a drill instructor, also known as a di, a Marine has to complete one term of enlistment and pass a psychological exam m to make sure they're not suffering from PTSD. If given the all clear, they attend an eleven week program where they learn how to teach recruits. In Jake Weaver's experience at Paris Island, there were essentially two training programs that ran parallel to one another. By day, recruits attended classes and completed tactical missions.

They completed grueling, physical exercises and other tasks that seemed pointless, like dangling rifles from their pinky fingers or sitting still for hours at a time. By night, an unofficial kind of training took place. Sometimes recruits weren't permitted to sleep. Drill instructors would pour detergent, shaving cream and other toiletries on the barracks floors and order recruits to run across it, while also scrubbing the floor with brushes. Jake would later tell journalist to Janet Reitman that the drill instructors referred disparagingly to what they called the New Corps. They felt that the

Marines had become too easy with the training being done by the book and no real struggle for the recruits it in Jake's experience, the dis saw it as their role to make Marines of them through hazing a process of degrading and abusing recruits as a form of initiation. There was a tacit understanding that what happened in the barracks stayed in the barracks.

As for Jake's own senior drill instructor, he was an erratic man who could be encouraging 1 minute and aggressive the next. Jake found the speed at which he lost his temper alarming. Under no circumstances were drill instructors permitted to touch recruits, yet this rule was often ignored. If a recruit was seen to be smiling or laughing, a di I might hit or choke them. The overexertion from the late night tasks they were forced to perform led to some recruits passing out or suffering a breakdown of skeletal muscle tissue. But none of them complained. During the first week of training, Jake Weaver's platoon listened to a talk by one of their drill instructors that focused on the fraternal connection between marines. All of them were brothers, the instructor said, regardless of their faith, ethnicity, or race. Then he asked each recruit what their religion was.

One of Jake's platoon mates was a young man from Brooklyn, New York, named Amir Bormesh. When he was asked which faith he followed, Amir replied, Islam, sir. The majority of the recruits were white men from Christian backgrounds. Many of them had never met a Muslim before, prompting the drill instructor to reassure everyone that there was nothing wrong with Amir's faith. But from that day on, Amir seemed to be singled out for harsher treatment than arrest. Intelligent and hardworking, he always performed well on every test. Yet the drill instructors made him undertake particularly grueling training sessions. On at least two occasions, Amir had to go to the medical unit after these incidents. One of the drill instructors from another platoon seemed to go out of his way to hassle Amir. He repeatedly called him a terrorist and asked him, Where are the WMDs? Were you part of 911? These questions were a reference to the

September 11, 2001, terrorist attacks on the United States by militant Islamic group Al Qaeda. The following the attacks the US Had gone to war against Iraq under the guise of looking for weapons of mass destruction.

Despite the ongoing harassment, Amir stuck with his training, and in early July of 2015, he and the other recruits completed their final task and officially became Marines. Late at night on July 14, 2015, the recruits in Platoon 30 54 were sleeping when the silence was suddenly broken by several men entering the squad bay. It was a number of the drill instructors, including the one who'd become fixated with Amir Bormesh. He was Gunnery Sergeant Joseph Felix. Sergeant Felix and his friends appeared to have been drinking. Making his way through the squad bay, Felix asked, Where's the terrorist? As he drew closer to Amir's bunk, he asked, you a terrorist? No, sir, Amir replied. You are Muslim, said Felix. Yes, sir. Answered Amir. Felix ordered him down. Then he and another di marched Amir towards the bathroom. Turning on the showers, they had a Mir lie down on the tiles and do pushups and other exercises. Amir Obediently did as he was told, getting soaked as water from the showerheads poured down on him. This sort of activity was known as incentive training on the spot physical training intended as a form of punishment. Eventually, told him to stop and took him to the laundry room. Get in the dryer, Felix ordered. He was referring to an industrial sized clothes dryer, big enough to fit a grown man. Amir, who was 6ft tall, climbed inside. I'm going to find out who you really are, said Felix before closing the dryer door. Who are you working for? He asked. Nobody. Sir, was Amir's reply? Displeased with this answer, Felix turned to the dryer on Amir's body tumbled inside as its drum began to turn. Back in the squad bay, the other recruits could hear the bang of Amir crashing against the bottom of the machine's interior. After about 30 seconds, Felix stopped the dryer and opened the door. What's your religion? He asked. Islam, sir. Said Amir. Felix closed the door and turned the dryer on again. You're going to kill us the first chance you get, aren't you, terrorist? What are your plans?

The inside of the dryer was starting to heat up, burning Amir's shoulder and neck. He began to cry. Once again. Felix stopped the dryer and demanded to know if Amir was still Muslim. When he said he was, the dryer was switched on again. Eventually, after the dryer had been turned on and off three times, Amir gave in and told them what they wanted to hear he was no longer a Muslim. After about 30 minutes, Amir was taken back to his bunk, still damp and visibly upset. Felix and his accomplice left and another dead eye went up to Amir. It's pretty feed up, what they did to you back there. You're not going to tell a senior drill instructor about this, though, right? No, sir, said Amir. The following night, Sergeant Joseph Felix returned to Platoon 3050. Four's squad bay. He made Amir hand over his martial arts belt and tied it around Amir's neck. He also tied Amir's shoelaces together and looped the belt through them, forcing Amir to bend a double, leading Amir around the bay as though he were a dog on a leash. Felix asked him, Are you a terrorist? Are you a spy? No, sir, cried Amir, who was in pain from the restraint. Yell laho Wakbar. Felix demanded. Amir did as he was told. Then Felix used a flagpole to push down on Amir's toes, crushing them before taking a different approach. Felix handed Amir a scrubbing brush and told him to behead a fellow recruit with it. Show us you're a terrorist. Amir hit the recruit's neck several times with the brush while crying out, Allah Akbar. An Arabic phrase that translates to God is the greatest. This seemed to make Felix happy. Amir's anxiety only increased in the days that followed. He also struggled with a loss of motivation. At night, he was plagued by nightmares that featured Felix killing his family. Amir wasn't the only recruit who was troubled. Jake Weaver struggled with some of the things he'd seen during training. And although he hadn't been targeted in the same way Amir had, he found himself grappling with mistreatment as well. On one occasion, a drill instructor pushed Jake's head against the wall. Another di had mocked him for being religious. Jake had high expectations of the Marines but was growing increasingly disillusioned about serving. His mental health began to suffer, and he wound up being hospitalized due to having suicidal thoughts. He decided to leave the Marines. To Jake's dismay, he found out he would be receiving an other than honorable discharge. A few months earlier, in May of 2015, an email had been sent to the Paris Island Recruit Depot. There was no name attached to it, with the author instead signing off as a retired Marine and a concerned parent. It read in part, I apologize for writing an anonymous email, but I do not want the drill instructors to mark my son for this email. As he is unaware that I am sending this. I am afraid I am going to be one of the parents who are very concerned about the treatment that the new Marines underwent at Third Recruit Training Battalion. I confirmed with my friends who were di's on Paris Island. And they agreed that you need to be aware of what is going on. The author went on to explain that his son had told him about his recent experiences while training. He and his fellow recruits had been told by their drill instructors that they didn't need blankets at night, as they were only for decoration. In an attempt to stay warm in the freezing cold barracks, the recruits slept in extra clothing and kept their hands tucked inside their shirts. One drill instructor in particular seemed to enjoy pushing recruits against a wall while choking their necks. The author's son had been shoved against the wall once and dislocated his shoulder. The recruits knew not to complain, having been told, what happens in Third

Battalion stays in Third Battalion. The author of the email clarified that he had been trained at Paris Island several decades earlier, as had his own father before him, but neither of them had ever experienced the kind of hazing that current recruits seemed to be enduring. Quote we both had hardcore di's, but not once did they ever touch us. Their style of leadership was absolutely awe-inspiring, sending shivers down our spines and filling our hearts with an overwhelming sense of pride and accomplishment, as if we had truly earned the prestigious title of Marine. The Third Battalion type of leadership will inevitably bring about devastating consequences for someone, and I can't help but feel deeply concerned about it.

20 year old Raheel Sadiqi was an unlikely marines recruit. The son of Pakistani immigrants, he had always been academically gifted rather than athletic. In his hometown of Taylor, Michigan. He was a star student at

Harry S. Truman High School. Raheel worked hard and barely socialized so that he could maintain perfect grades. He consulted his school's guidance counselor on what would be the most challenging classes to take. His dream was to study engineering at college. Raheel saw how hard his parents worked, his father at an auto parts factory and his mother picking up odd jobs. He wanted to help support them. When he graduated high school, Raheel was a valedictorian and 9th in his class overall. Raheel was accepted at multiple universities and was even offered a full scholarship to Michigan State. Then, in April 2014, he found out that he'd been accepted at the University of Michigan Dearborn, a college with a robotics engine nearing program Raheel was particularly drawn to. They weren't providing a full scholarship, but were offering a $2,000.01 as well as financial aid. This meant his parents wouldn't have to pay expensive college tuition as long as Raheel kept his grades above a C average. Raheel was ambitious and so decided to aim even higher. He enrolled in the college's honors program, which would require him to maintain a B average. As well as studying hard, Raheel worked part time on the service desk of a Home Depot store, a home improvement franchise. When he finished high school, he decided to work longer hours so he could provide his parents with financial support. Raheel wanted there to be enough money so his younger sister could one day go to college too. He started working 20 hours a week. Juggling work and study was harder than Raheel had anticipated. He began to feel stressed about the amount of pressure he was under to maintain top grades. By the end of his first semester, Raheel started getting C's instead of the A's he was used to. In July 2015, the summer after Raheel's freshman year, he surprised his parents with an announcement he was leaving college and enlisting with the Marines. His mother, Ghazala, and father Massoud were shocked. Raheel had never expressed any interest in the military, and they couldn't understand why he was abandoning his long held dream of being at college. He reassured them that this was a way that he could serve his country and would also allow him to achieve his dreams. Recruiters had told him that he could continue his studies while serving. Plus, he'd already chosen a technical specialty working on marine aircraft, which meant he probably wouldn't have to fight unless he wanted to down the track. His experience could even help him pursue a career with the FBI. Raheel described the chance to serve as a golden opportunity, adding, after three years in the Marine Corps, I can do anything. Raheel encouraged his worried mother to visit the marines recruitment office in Taylor so she could speak to the recruiters herself. Ghazala did so and was reassured by the marines that her son would be entirely safe. Recruiters were prevalent in the part of Michigan where the Sadiqi family lived. Located about 15 miles southwest of Detroit, Taylor was known as one of the downriver communities, and there were three military recruiting stations in the area. When the state's auto manufacturing industry declined, so did the area's socioeconomic standing. In Taylor, 15% of residents live below the poverty line. For young people in need of a career, the military can be an appealing option. And for the Marines, highly intelligent, hardworking individuals such as Raheel Sadiqi are ideal recruits. By July 8, 2015, Raheel Sadiqi had signed his enlistment papers and began the Marine's delayed entry program. The program would introduce Raheel to the marine's culture with meetings every Saturday. Embracing his new path wholeheartedly, Raheel began preparing for training. He woke up every morning at 04:00 a.m. To work out at the gym. He learned how to swim. He installed exercise equipment at home so he could also work out there. And he began drinking protein shakes. Raheel's family was astonished at the changes in him. He had always been academically driven, but now he was physically motivated as well. His recruiter told them how impressed he was by Raheel's work ethic. He was definitely the most driven recruit of the lot. Finally, after eight months, Raheel's time to attend boot camp at Paris island arrived. His parents remained nervous. Raheel had never even stayed away from home for a single night before, and now he would be spending several months interstate with total strangers. Ghazala Sadiqi had a nagging feeling that going away wasn't the right thing for her son. But when she asked him one last time if he was 100% sure, he replied, no, mum, it's okay. I made up my mind. I'm ready to go. Don't worry about me. He promised to adhere to the teachings of their Islamic faith while away and follow Muslim dietary requirements as best as possible. In February 2016, Raheel's colleagues at Home Depot threw him a goodbye party. They all knew Raheel as someone who was highly intelligent, but not the most street smart. Some were worried that his outlook was too positive. He was a kind person who couldn't conceive of anyone being unkind. One of his friends warned him be careful. Just watch yourself. You don't know what kinds of people are down there. You don't know how other people think. On Sunday, March 6, 2016, refill said goodbye to his parents and sister, promising to call when he arrived at Paris Island for the next day, Ghazala and Massoud waited patiently for the phone to ring. Finally, late at night on Monday, March 7, it rang. Ghazala quickly answered it and was met with very strange sounds. It sounded like indecipherable grunting and shouting set against a noisy background. After less than 5 seconds, the line went dead. Ghazala said her son's name, but there was no reply. You Ghazala were worried. The call hadn't sounded like Raheel at all. The next morning, she contacted Raheel's recruiter and shared her concerns, stating no one knows my son's voice better than me. That didn't sound like my son. The recruiter reassured her that all was fine. Raheel had arrived safely at the base. He'd just sounded strange because he'd been reading the script that all recruits had to follow when they first called home and only had a few seconds to do it. But Ghazala Sadiqi couldn't shake the feeling that something was wrong. When Raheel Sadiqi arrived at Paris Island alongside around 4000 other recruits laid on Monday, March 7 he followed the same instructions that all new recruits followed. After four days of administrative tasks and strength tests he was assigned to Platoon 3042. On

Saturday, March 12, platoon 3042 sat within Kilo company in the third battalion. Kilo Company is known amongst the drill instructors and recruits as Killer Kilo. A nod to its intensity, Raheel and his 58 platoon mates were taken to their squad bay. It sat on the third floor of its building and was about 60 yards long and 15 yards wide. Two long rows of bunk beds flanked two walls with a wide aisle down the middle. The recruits were instructed to sit cross-legged on the floor. Their senior drill instructor introduced himself. It was Gunnery Sergeant Joseph Felix who had been reassigned from the platoon he'd had the previous year. Speaking in a harsh, authoritative tone Felix promised to treat his new recruits with firmness, fairness, dignity and compassion. Under no circumstances would abuse be tolerated. Then the real training began. Recruits had to jump on each other in a dog pile, then run back and forth. They were made to do hundreds of burpees, a full body exercise where they dropped to a pushup, then jumped in the air. They had to dangle their rifles from their little fingers. Even the extremely fit recruits found it excruciating. One later told journalist To Janet Reitman of the New York Times that thought he would pass out. Another recruit had a panic attack and started vomiting. At first, officers were supervising from the back of the room. After they left, the drill instructors only intensified the training. The next morning, at 07:20 a.m., the recruits had already been up and training for several hours.

When Raheel Sadiqi reported that he wanted to die, his instructors pushed back against this, asking him what his mother would think if he left before finishing training. Raheel replied, I'd tell my mother goodbye and kill myself. The future does not matter. This recruit is going to kill himself. He'd even figured out how he would do it. He would jump from the squad bay window. Realizing that they were dealing with the suicide threat, the drill instructors confiscated Raheel's belt and the laces from his boots. Military police were summoned and arrived within minutes. As it wasn't unusual for recruits to threaten self-harm in the early days of their training, the marines had a strict protocol they followed. When the military police spoke with Raheel, he elaborated on what had upset him. He couldn't handle drill instructors yelling at him and hitting him. The instructors dismissed Raheel's claims. They hadn't hit him. They had only touched him when they had to provide corrections, such as fixing his uniform or position. Drill instructors were barred from touching recruits in all situations except drill corrections. It was determined that Raheel should remain on the base under suicide watch. Recruits were only transported off base treatment if they had actually self-harmed or attempted suicide. Raheel was moved to another platoon squad bay and was told to sit on a mattress in the middle of the room. He sat there for 24 hours while other recruits took it in turns to watch over him. When night fell, they shone a torch into his face in order to keep an eye on him. Eventually, Raheel spoke up and said he'd changed his mind. He didn't want to die at all. He wanted to continue training and become a Marine. The next morning, Raheel's senior drill instructor, Gunnery Sergeant Joseph Felix, took Raheel to recruit liaison services to discuss the previous day's events with a higher up. Usually drill instructors waited outside for recruits for meetings like this, but Felix stayed in the office throughout, about 10ft away from Raheel. Raheel explained that he had no intention of killing himself and had no history of mental health problems. He had only said that because he wanted the training to stop. But quote this recruit thought it was the only way to quit. The recruit never meant that and regrets it. Raheel was dismissed as a low risk for self-harm and returned to his platoon. Over the next few days, the recruits continued training. They had to perform sprints and cross country runs. They were taught mixed martial arts, bayonet techniques and close order drills. During one routine focused on punching, recruits were split into pairs and instructed to punch one another repeatedly. Many of the larger, stronger recruits were teamed up. Smaller individuals. They were told not to listen to their di's instructions, just to keep punching. Many recruits were hid in their jaws. One suffered broken ribs. Another broke down in tears. Drill instructors would refer to their recruits as maggots pussies and a variety of sexist and homophobic slurs. Some were targeted for their personal attributes, such as their ethnicity. Drill instructors themselves weren't immune from abuse either. Senior di's would often yell at their subordinates, who in turn took out their anger on recruits. After Gunnery Sergeant Joseph Felix shouted at one di, he began screaming at his recruits to the extent that he became sick and vomited across the floor. One of Raheel Sadiqi's platoon mates noticed that Raheel seemed baffled by being asked to follow orders. Following orders was crucial to being in the Marines, but Raheel seemed to query why he was being told to do certain things. His platoon mate wondered why he had enlisted it and later told the New York Times that Raheel always looked like a scared animal. At about 02:00 a.m. On Friday, March 18, the recruit who shared Raheel's bunk was woken by Raheel. He wanted to talk to him, explaining that he was in pain. We're all in pain, his bunk mate replied before turning over to go back to sleep. 2 hours later, it was time for the recruits to get up. By 415, they were lined up to go to breakfast. A drill instructor told them to sound off before they left, a term used for the call marines are required to give in response to an order. All except Raheel obeyed. Two di's noticed and began to yell at him for disobeying orders. When one approached Raheel and demanded, he sounded off. Raheel pointed at his throat and silently passed him a note. It read this recruit has to go to medical. The swelling in this recruit's throat has persisted for three days. This recruit lost his voice entirely yesterday night, and he can barely whisper because he coughed blood several times. This enlistee's entire neck is in excruciating pain. After breakfast, Raheel's drill teacher would handle the situation. Raheel would have to join the rest of his unit at the meal hall in the meanwhile. At breakfast, a drill instructor asked for Raheel's help. Passing out cups, Raheel ignored him. He sat quietly as the rest of the platoon ate, staring into space. You by 05:30 a.m. The platoon was back at their barracks, doing some cleaning. Raheel was ordered to the front of the squad bay so he could fill out a form to go to the medical unit when Raheel approached Senior Drill Instructor Joseph Felix Raheel didn't address him as was required. Presumably due to his sore throat. Instead, he stood there silently. Felix became angry and demanded, Raheel, run. Get backs across the squad bay. This involved sprinting back and forth across the length of the room until told to stop. Exercise such as this was known as incentive training in Raheel did as he was told while holding his throat as Felix continued to shout Sadiqi, run. Get back. Run. I don't care what's wrong with you. You're going to say something back to me. The other recruits kept cleaning quietly as Raheel ran back and forth across the squad bay. Then suddenly, Raheel clutched his throat and fell to the floor, crying. He lay there motionless, his hands still wrapped around his neck. Get up, Saidik I know you're faking. Yelled Felix. Get up. He walked over to Reheel and slapped him across the face. Reheel's head turned to one side, but otherwise he didn't move. Felix slapped him again. He did it so forcefully that the sound echoed across the enormous squad bay. Raheel stood up, holding his face, and began running again. One of his platoon mates thought it was the fastest he'd ever seen anyone run before. He it looked as though Raheel was completing the get backs he'd been ordered to do, but then he kept running to the back of the room, where a set of double doors led to an external staircase. Raheel pushed the doors open and hoisted himself up on the railing of the stairway. Then his feet caught on the metal rail and he tumbled over the side. At 05:35, A.m., a marine who happened to be outside passing by saw Raheel's body fall from the third floor and hit the concrete below. The marine called 911 and reported, I got a recruit that fell from the third deck. Meanwhile, up in the squad bay, Raheel's shocked. Platoon mates were ordered to file into the bathroom and face the wall. While Raheel was being given first aid, they were taken to complete their usual training schedule. Drill instructors warned them not to talk about what they'd seen. Raheel had suffered severe blunt force trauma but was still alive. An air ambulance was requested to take him to a hospital 40 miles away. Due to heavy fog, an airlift wasn't possible, so the marines drove Raheel to Buford Memorial Hospital. For an hour, emergency room doctors worked on Raheel. They realized that he needed a more specialized form of care, so he was transferred to another hospital in Charleston.

Ghazala Sadiqi hadn't stopped worrying about her son since he left home for boot camp. She'd only had one bizarre phone call from him and hadn't been able to talk to him at all. At 07:00 p.m. On Friday, March 18, a week and a half after that call, there was a knock on the front door of the Sadiqi residence. Ghazala answered the door to see two Marines standing outside. Ghazala assumed they must be there to share some good news about her son's achievements at training. The thought was a relief. She had been worried about Raheel since he'd gone away, to the extent that she'd struggled to sleep at night. Ghazala invited the Marines inside. The two officers stepped inside and asked if everyone was at home. Ghazala said that she and her daughter Sidra were there, but her husband, Massoud, was at work. One of the officers stepped back outside and made a brief phone call. As he was talking,

Sidra overheard him say, the dad's not home now. Should I still say it? Sidra was confused and couldn't understand what was happening. The officer returned and said to Ghazala, ma'am, I have bad news. Your son passed away. In total disbelief, Ghazala replied, no, no, you're wrong. You're wrong. Something is wrong. Then she cried out for Sidra to call her father before fainting. When Gazala woke, she was in the hospital being treated for shock. Despite the best efforts of doctors in South Carolina, Raheel had been pronounced dead at ten 06:00 a.m. Four and a half hours after his fall. His death was ruled a suicide almost a week later, on Thursday, March 24, Raheel's body was flown home to Michigan in a coffin draped with an American flag. When the Sadiqi family viewed his body at the funeral home, they were horrified by what they saw. There were ligature marks around his neck and most of his body had a purplish hue. When the family read Raheel's autopsy report, they noticed that in addition to the blunt force trauma, the forensic pathologist found evidence of particular hemorrhaging. This could be caused by heavy coughing or vomiting or even strangulation. Despite the coroner's ruling of suicide, the Sadiqis couldn't believe Raheel had taken his own life. That they felt his devotion to his parents would make it impossible for him to do so, as well as his Islamic faith, which considered suicide a sin. Certain there was more to the situation than met the eye. They retained a lawyer to advocate on their behalf. When officials interviewed the Sadiqis, they confirmed that Raheel had no history of mental illness. He had always been well behaved, with a mischievous sense of humor, and their memory of him was as a son who smiled all the time. Upon hearing the story of how Raheel had died, the Sadiqis and their lawyer were unsettled. They couldn't understand how so many witnesses in the squad bay had seen Raheel collapse and be slapped by Felix. Yet only one individual had detailed how he had fallen. An investigation into Raheel's death began. It was coordinated by the Paris Island office of the Naval Criminal Investigative Service, also known as NCIS. While they were adamant that there were no indications of foul play, they still wanted to gain a full understanding of the events that led up to Raheel's death. Although the investigation would look at Paris Island as a whole, it was primarily focused on the Third Recruit Training Battalion. Much of the investigation's focus was on Gunnery Sergeant Joseph Felix, who had been Raheel's senior drill instructor. Aged in his 30s, Felix had enlisted in the Marines in two two. During his 14 years of service, he had worked as an air traffic controller and was deployed to the Iraq and Afghanistan wars. His time there left a lasting impact on him. Felix would rant to other Marines about how he hated Muslims. Blame, blaming them for killing friends who'd served alongside him. While it is unclear whether Joseph Felix suffered PTSD following his service in war zones, one officer told the New York Times he had a reputation for being, quote, pretty frickin'psycho one of the more aggressive drill instructors in his company. He even scared recruits who weren't in his platoon. One recruit who'd been training in Raheel Sadiqi's cohort saw Felix push another recruit into a foot Locker. Others were choked or thrown against walls. On one occasion, Felix forced a recruit to only eat jelly and mashed potatoes for several days. And it appeared that Felix had a history of singling out Muslim recruits. In particular, in 2015, the year before Raheel Sadiqi began training, Felix had repeatedly tormented a young Muslim from Brooklyn named Amir Bormesh. As well as accusing him of being a terrorist spy, Felix forced Amir into an industrial dryer, then turned it on. And Amir wasn't the only victim. That same year, Felix honed in on a 19 year old named Rakhan Harwaz. Rakhan had immigrated to the United States from Kurdistan with his family. As a baby, Felix nicknamed Rakhan terrorist ISIS and Kurdish. Like Amir, Rakhan was forced into a dry by Felix, although he didn't switch it on. Despite the ethos of what happens in Third Battalion stays in Third Battalion, these incidents hadn't gone unreported. When recruit Jake Weaver was told in 2015 that he would be receiving an other than honorable discharge from the Marines, his father decided to step in. Troy Weaver had been told by his son about the abuses that had gone on at Paris Island. It seemed incredibly unfair that Jake would be receiving a bad discharge after what he'd seen and experienced. Troy Weaver contacted Jake's commanding officer and shared what he knew.

This got the ball rolling. A code of silence had prevented recruits from speaking up earlier. But after Troy Weaver reached out, the Marines opened an investigation into the allegations. On November 5, 2015, Jake Weaver provided a statement, as did Amir Bormesh. Two months later, the findings were submitted. The training regiment's executive officer found the evidence compelling enough for the drill instructors involved to be stood down from their duties, including Joseph Felix, but no action followed. Four months later, Joseph Felix was given the role of senior drill instructor for Platoon 3042. Raheel Sadiqi, a Pakistani American Muslim, was assigned to this platoon, despite Felix's history of abusing Islamic recruits. On Thursday, March 17, 2016, an individual involved in the 2015 Hays investigation contacted the investigating officer to suggest more witnesses be interviewed. An email had just arrived from someone corroborating some of the most serious allegations. The following day was the day that Reheel died. Many of the recruits from Raheel's platoon noticed how Gunnery Sergeant Joseph Felix seemed to single Raheel out. Some heard him call Raheel a terrorist again and again in a completely serious tone. One recruit estimated that in just a few days of training, Felix addressed Raheel as a terrorist more than ten times. Times in one meeting, he told Raheel that he smelled like a terrorist. At another, Felix asked the recruits if any of them knew what a bazaar was. Raheel said that he did. Of course you do, you goddamn terrorist, Felix replied. He also asked him if he needed his turban. At least one of the other recruits noticed that Raheel seemed reluctant to obey Felix's commands after being spoken to this way. Just the day after joining Felix's platoon, Raheel mentioned wanting to kill himself. Felix attended a meeting where Raheel discussed what he'd said. Even though it was usual protocol for drill instructors to wait outside such meetings, reports as to what exactly occurred in the immediate lead up to Raheel's death were mixed. Some of his platoon mates who'd witnessed Felix reprimanding him said Felix had ordered Raheel to run while choking his own throat. Others thought Raheel was holding his throat because it was sore. One witness said he'd seen Felix throw Raheel to the floor. The others all believed Raheel had collapsed on his own. Everyone agreed that Felix had slapped Raheel, but some thought he did so only once to revive him. Others said Felix slapped him hard two or three times. After that, Raheel had leapt up and sprinted out of the squad bay and over a stairwell. He died just five days after being assigned to Felix's platoon. On Thursday, September 8, 2016, six months after Raheel's death, the Marines released a 133 page report about the matter and other allegations of abuse. Much of it was redacted with 40 pages completely blacked out. Nevertheless, it was clear the Marines had concluded that the actions of Joseph Felix directly led to Raheel jumping from the building. They also stated that Felix should never have been assigned to Raheel's platoon, given he was already under investigation for harassing another Muslim recruit. It was recommended that Felix be charged with assault for slapping Raheel. The report also focused on incidents involving other recruits being choked and forced to engage in unauthorized incentive training.

It found Marines working as drill instructors had been operating with impunity without the proper supervision or leadership. 20 Marines were relieved of duty in the wake of the investigation, including three teams of drill instructors and the depot's regimental commander. Four were charged for incidents of abuse unrelated to Raheel Sadiqi joseph Felix was charged with failure to obey a general order, cruelty and maltreatment, making a false statement, and drunk and disorderly conduct. Raheel's family was disappointed with the charges. They didn't understand why Felix wasn't charged with assault, as the report had recommended. Joseph Felix was ordered to face a military trial which began in November 2017. The trial would not center on the death of Raheel Sadiqi, but focus on numerous allegations regard Felix's treatment of recruits. The prosecution called almost 70 witnesses to the stand. Other drill instructors testified about behavior they'd witnessed from Felix. Various recruits spoke of him choking them, hitting them against walls and forcing them to hurt one another. The prosecution also detailed how Felix had seemingly targeted Muslim recruits, describing his actions as hate crimes. Amir Bormesh and Rakhan Havaz spoke of how Felix had abused them for being Muslim, with both of them being forced into industrial dryers. Amir said Felix had tumbled him in the dryer for up to 30 seconds at a time. An expert on industrial dryers confirmed that a model such as the one in the Third Battalion's laundry was large enough to hold and tumble a recruit weighing up to 168 pounds. The defense only called one expert witness a burns expert. She said that in 30 seconds, the dryer would have reached temperatures over 300 degrees Fahrenheit, or 149 degrees Celsius. This would have caused third or fourth degree burns within 1 second. Yet Amir had no physical evidence of burns.

However. The expert did acknowledge that shorter durations could still cause pain without leaving visible injuries, adding, if I were in a dryer, 3 seconds would seem like an eternity. Although some said Felix spoke openly about his dislike of Muslims, Felix's lawyer insisted that his client hadn't specifically targeted Muslim recruits. He had only discussed the Islamic faith with Amir out of curiosity, and he had chosen Rakhan Havez to be squad leader after discovering he was Muslim. Some witnesses suggested that Felix had only called Muslim recruits terrorists as a joke and hadn't meant anything by it at all. The eight person jury, made up of male Marines, spent a day deliberating before reaching a verdict. They found Felix guilty of eight counts of violating training orders regarding multiple recruits, including slapping Raheel and forcing him to sprint laps while sick. But he was found not guilty of referring to Raheel as a terrorist. Felix was also convicted for being drunk and disorderly and making false official statements. But he was cleared of obstructing justice for supposedly telling recruits to conceal information about what happened to Raheel. During his sentencing, Joseph Felix addressed the court. He apologized to his wife, stating, thank you for standing by me and being as wonderful as you are. I can never repay the disappointment I feel you have in me. He did not apologize to the Sadiqi family or the other recruits he had abused. Nor did he acknowledge any of the charges he'd been convicted of. Felix's attorney asked that his client only serve 30 days in prison, while the prosecution asked for seven years. He was sentenced to ten years. His rank would also be reduced. He would have to forfeit all pay and allowances and would subsequently be given a dishonorable discharge. A total of five Marines ended up being convicted or pleading guilty to charges relating to hazing of recruits of Paris Island. Raheel Sadiqi's death wasn't the first time a recruit died at the depot. In 1956, a drill instructor ordered his platoon to march across a swamp. Six recruits drowned. Two decades later, another recruit was beaten with training sticks and subsequently died. Raheel's death had a ripple effect throughout the United States. Then President Barack Obama had his attention drawn to the case. A Democratic Congresswoman from Detroit reached out to the Sadiqis and petitioned the Marines on their behalf for an unbiased inquiry into hazing. In the wake of Raheel's death, Marine Corps Commandant General Robert Nella, the highest ranking official in the Marines, stated, we mourn the loss of recruit Sadiqi, and we will take every step necessary to prevent tragic events like this from happening again. One of Raheel's platoon mates told the New York Times that despite some changes to training, he and the other recruits were still treated badly even after Raheel's death. Let's say you did report something, he said. They changed the di. And what happens after that? Another di who presumably was friends with the prior di is going to make your life hell. Several months after Reheel died, a new commanding general was appointed to the Paris Islander Depot. Austin Renforth set about making changes; including having officers supervise drill instructors more actively and updating a policy letter to emphasize the Marine's zero tolerance approach to Hazing. In an interview with the New York Times, he admitted that he'd thought about contacting Raheel's parents but decided, quote I just didn't feel it was my place. The Sadiqis struggled with the silence they received from the Marines after Reheel died. His sister Sidra told the Detroit Free Press newspaper that she now had difficulty saying the Pledge of Allegiance a patriotic verse that student's at most American public schools have to recite. Her faith in the country her parents had immigrated to for a better life had been broken. The Sadiqis chose not to speak to most reporters as they were disappointed with the way their son had been portrayed in the media as though he were weak or unprepared for boot camp. In order to be accepted as a recruit, he'd had to pass a psychological exam. None of them had ever witnessed nest any signs pointing to Raheel having a mental illness or suicidal thoughts. They remain convinced that Raheel would never take his own life and believe there are unanswered questions relating to his death. That the family lodged a civil suit suing the federal government for $100 million for their son's death. Their lawyer was arguing that the marines had been negligent when recruiting Raheel. In failing to tell him there had been allegations of abuse against Muslim recruits at Paris Island. At a time when the marine corps was eager to attract recruits from more diverse backgrounds, it seemed they had a duty of care to ensure those recruits would be safe from possible hate crimes. The Sadiqis also wanted Raheel's death certificate amended. A coroner had marked his cause of death as suicide, but his family thought it should be listed as undetermined. Because of the way Raheel's feet tripped over the stairwell, causing him to fall awkwardly, it wasn't clear whether he had truly intended to take his own life. Perhaps he'd just been trying to escape. Joseph Felix the lawsuit was ultimately dismissed due to a federal precedent that prevents the US. Government from being sued for harm to military personnel. The judge who made the ruling said he had no other option and expressed strong reservations about having to do so. The Sadiqis have retained Raheel's bedroom as a kind of shrine to him. It has been kept perfectly clean and is dotted with awards that Raheel won for his academic achievements. And hanging in the closet is a reminder of what he wanted to achieve the perfectly pressed dress uniform that Raheel would have worn upon graduating from training with the marines.